FROM WORDS OF WOE TO UNBELIEVABLE NEWS

ALTERNATIVE VOICES FOR THE LENTEN JOURNEY

ROBERT D. CORNWALL

Topical Line Drives, Volume 19

INTRODUCTION BY DAVID ACKERMAN

Energion Publications
Gonzalez, FL
2015

ISBN10: 1-63199-141-8
ISBN13: 978-1-63199-141-7

Energion Publications
P. O. Box 841
Gonzalez, FL 32560

energionpubs.com
pubs@energion.com
850-525-3916

PREFACE

I am a preacher and on most Sundays during the year you will find me in the pulpit sharing a message that I hope and pray will bring a word from God to the congregation. On a majority of Sundays I turn to the *Revised Common Lectionary* for a text to share. I do this for a number of reasons, including its connection to the liturgical year. There's another reason, however, why I like to use the lectionary. Because I seek to be a biblical preacher, the lectionary gives me the opportunity to sit with a text and ask of it what word God might have for me and the congregation. The lectionary takes us to a wide variety of texts in both Testaments, but if we stick too closely to the RCL we will leave a great swath of scripture unexplored.

When Bruce Epperly introduced me to David Ackerman, a pastor from the United Church of Christ who had created his own fourth year lectionary, I was intrigued. Here was a set of texts that could take me to new places. For the past year I've been posting David's worship materials and sermon starters on my blog. I made use of these texts for the first time as the foundation for sermons during Advent and Christmas season of 2013. This first venture took me to places like the Book of Daniel and stories that are well known, but rarely preached. When I was looking at what to preach during Lent, I decided to take a look at David's lectionary. As I did so, I decided to use his readings from the Gospels for the Sundays of Lent through Easter Sunday. Some of these texts are rather dark and challenging. If you read these texts you might get a sense why they weren't included in the RCL. For instance, some of them exhibit anti-Jewish tendencies. Still, they're part of the canon. Even passages like the longer ending of Mark, which most scholars have deemed a late addition and not originally part of Mark, have been considered Scripture by the Church. So is there a message in a text like that?

I'm pleased to share these sermons, preached during Lent through Easter Sunday 2014, for your consideration. I'm also pleased that David agreed to write an introduction to these sermons, sharing his rationale for developing this lectionary and how my sermons illustrate what he was hoping to see happen as preachers step out of the comfort zone provided by the RCL and take up texts rarely explored, at least in most Mainline Protestant congregations.

I want to thank David for his contributions to this enterprise. I also wish to thank my publishers — Henry and Jody Neufeld for providing me with a platform to share my journey of faith through the written word. Finally, I must extend words of gratitude to the parishioners of Central Woodward Christian Church (Disciples of Christ) for inviting me to serve as their pastor and their preacher, and thus allowing me to take up these texts.

Robert D. Cornwall
Easter 2014

INTRODUCTION

For fifteen years as a local church pastor, I religiously preached on the readings of the *Revised Common Lectionary* (*RCL*). I did so for several reasons. I loved the fact that the readings conformed so well to the rhythms of the liturgical year. I valued the discipline of preaching from pre-selected texts instead of choosing my own based on my feelings at a given moment. I loved the ecumenical character of the lectionary and took comfort in thinking that people in different churches could "compare notes" on how the same scriptures were creatively used in their respective congregations. But after going through five three-year cycles of the *RCL*, I felt that there was much of the Bible that I was never sharing from the pulpit.

So I crunched the numbers. It turns out that the *RCL* uses just under 25 percent of the Bible on Sundays and mainline Protestant holy days. This leaves more than 75 percent of scripture that *RCL* users may never address from the pulpit. When I awoke to this fact, I was curious about the content that was omitted. As I began to explore the passages that the *RCL* overlooked, I found many of them to be both amazing and inspiring. I found other readings, however, to be difficult and deeply challenging. These are often the focus scriptures of the culture wars of our day, and unless preachers address them from the pulpit, they risk the prospect that parishioners will simply take them at face value, without adequately considering their social context. As a progressive Christian pastor, I am deeply concerned that the interpretation of these passages will become the domain of fundamentalists, who will contort them to fit an untenably narrow worldview, or atheists, who will attempt to depict the Bible as a book of horrors. As I considered my desire to exercise the use of scripture in worship more fully, I wondered if a year's worth of readings, following the selection pattern of the *RCL*, could be gleaned from the remaining parts of the Bible. I began to craft such a lectionary, tailoring readings from the Hebrew Scriptures, Psalms, Epistles/New Testament, and Gospels in such a way that they conformed to the patterns of the church year. The end result of my work is *Beyond the Lectionary: A Year of Alternatives to the Revised Common Lectionary* (Circle, 2013).

Over the past couple years there has been a gratifying response to this effort. The cover of October 30, 2013 *Christian Century* asks, "Which Lectionary?" and the article, "A Wealth of Lectionaries," mentions the book (p. 27). While it has also been cited in other publications (e.g., *Lutheran Forum*, Winter, 2013, p. 23) and used in various settings in both America and Europe, perhaps the most gratifying response I have received has come from Disciples of Christ pastor, Dr. Robert Cornwall. After hearing about Bob through our mutual friend, Dr. Bruce Epperly, I introduced myself to him by asking if he would be willing to mention my book on his blog, "Ponderings on a Faith Journey." At the time, I had no idea how graciously he would eventually open up space to me, not only on his blog, but also in his life and ministry.

One of the things I quickly learned and came to admire about Bob is how capably he wears so many hats. As a theologian, historian, pastor and author, Bob has successfully integrated a vast diversity of skills in his ministry. Holding a Ph.D. in historical theology from Fuller Theological Seminary, Bob is both a voracious reader and prolific writer. He has authored eight books and is the Editor of the Academy of Parish Clergy's journal — *Sharing the Practice.* Since 2008, he has served as Senior Pastor of the historic Central Woodward Christian Church in Troy, Michigan. How he manages all of these roles while maintaining such an appetite for theological adventure is amazing to me! Yet Bob indeed is driven to such exploration, which is how he came to embrace my lectionary and use it in new and transformative ways.

The book that is before you, *From Words of Woe to Unbelievable News*, is a product of that spirit of adventure. Bob takes the risk of stepping outside of the familiar comforts of the *Revised Common Lectionary* and explores the readings that I propose in *Beyond the Lectionary*. The season of Lent, I believe, is a particularly good time to do this because the readings in this season are especially challenging. They show how Lent may be understood not simply as a time for individual discipline but for corporate repentance as well. In ways that go beyond isolated individuals giving up certain foods or practices, the season of Lent challenges Christians to work for social justice as an expression of faith on a deeply communal level. To that end, the texts that I chose point to ways in which Christians have misused the Bible to exclude or even commit violence against others. In seminars where I have presented the book, I have described the Lenten texts as an "Olympics" of preaching. The readings are not for the timid or faint of heart and require a creative approach to bridging the cultural gap between the context of Biblical world and ours. In these sermons, which Bob preached at Central Woodward Christian Church in Lent of 2014, he shows himself to be more than capable of pulling off this task.

In his sermons for the five regular Sundays in Lent, Bob takes on this challenge in ways that evoked both my admiration and surprise.

- On the first Sunday of Lent, in "Words of Woe," Bob preaches on Matthew 23:27-36 and rightly notes how "Christians have a history of using passages like this to demonize and brutalize Jews." He then goes on to show how all of us, particularly those of us in religious leadership, are guilty of hypocrisy and must constantly strive to be in tune with our authentic selves.
- In "No Signs for You" on Lent 2, Bob focuses on Matthew 12:38-42 and discusses how Jesus uses the sign of Jonah not only as a metaphor for his death and resurrection but also as a warning against those who oppress and exclude the most vulnerable members of society.
- The sermon for Lent 3, "A Time to Weep," has its basis in Luke 19:41-44 and illustrates the hurt and anger that Jesus feels because Jerusalem has not recognized "the things that make for peace (v 42)" and "the time of [its] visitation (v 44)." Bob offers a similar lament for the city of Detroit today, citing current injustices perpetrated both within and against the city.
- On Lent 4 in "Difficult Paths," Bob connects the prophecy of Jesus' death (Mark 10:32-34) to hardships and injustices faced by his parishioners. He cites Irenaeus' recapitulation theory of atonement as a way of showing that God shares both in our

suffering and in the path that ultimately leads us to divine wholeness.

- The final regular Lenten Sunday, "Be Alert," is based on Mark 13:21-23. It addresses Jesus' warning against false teachers and calls us to practice "good religion," which "defines our witness to our neighbors" and necessarily reflects an authentic position of justice.

The last two sermons are based on scriptures that are personal favorites of mine. "Time's Up" is the Palm/Passion Sunday message, and it's rooted in John 16:16-33. Bob creatively explores the imagery of verses 21-22, where Jesus compares what will happen to him to the act of childbirth. This image of birth and new life carries over into Bob's final sermon, "Unbelievable News." Most scholars believe that the resurrection account in Mark 16:9-16 is a later addition to the gospel. As a result, it is omitted by the *RCL* and is rarely used by mainline Christian preachers. Still, Bob uses it here to show how impossible it is to domesticate the resurrection. There is something about it that cannot be tamed and must be relegated to the domain of mystery. It is news that we are called to proclaim with our lives, and, as Bob puts it in his conclusion, "If we're willing to take a risk and follow the risen Christ into the heart of God, then we will get to participate in an insurrection that can change the world!"

As you begin this journey through Lent with Dr. Robert Cornwall, expect the unexpected. Anticipate surprises along the way as he engages the scripture in new and dramatic ways. The journey may be difficult at times, especially when you encounter the words of woe. But it ends with unbelievable news — news that sounds too good to be true. Yet it is.

David J. Ackerman,
Conference Minister of the Penn West Conference,
United Church of Christ
May 2014

CHAPTER 1
WORDS OF WOE

Matthew 23:27-36

Can we find good news in words of woe? If you're a fan of a softer, gentler, smiling hippy Jesus who preaches peace and love — all the time — then you might be glad that the Revised Common Lectionary tends to skip over texts like Matthew 23. But, as we begin our Lenten journey, I decided to turn once again to David Ackerman's alternative lectionary,[1] which invites us to consider some of the darker and heavier texts in Scripture. The season of Lent is a good time to hear texts like this. Lent invites us to consider the darker side of our lives. In Matthew 23, Jesus offers seven "words of woe," two of which we've heard read for us this morning.

This word of judgment comes after Jesus' triumphal entry into Jerusalem. The crowd that gathered around Jesus is excited. They're hoping Jesus will turn the tables on their oppressors — just like he turned the tables on the marketers in the Temple. He's already debated one group of religious leaders — the Sadducees. Now he addresses a group of legal scholars and holiness preachers who'd come to take him on. Jesus responds to their challenge with a seven-point sermon, in which each point begins: "Woe to you Scribes and Pharisees, Hypocrites." As I read this passage, a song from *Godspell* came to mind. Maybe you remember it.

> *Alas alas for you Lawyers and Pharisees*
> *Hypocrites that you be*
> *Searching for souls and fools to forsake them*
> *You travel the land you scour the sea*
> *After you've got your converts you make them*
> *Twice as fit for hell! As you are yourselves!*

As the song continues, Jesus mentions the prophets whom God sends, but whom they ignore and even kill. It's a hard driving melody that brings out the intensity with which Jesus confronted

---

1   David Ackerman, *Beyond the Lectionary*, (Circle Books, 2013).

the religious leaders of his day — and perhaps religious leaders of our day.

According to Jesus, these religious leaders are like whitewashed tombs — pretty on the outside, but nothing more than a pile of rotting bones on the inside. It seems that they're hoping they can cover the foulness of spiritual death that envelops them with monuments to the very prophets they murder.

Of course, if you read on from here, you will discover that Good Friday is only a few days in the future. Because they won't own up to their own complicity in these earlier acts of violence, they will continue the tradition by murdering the one who is speaking to them. The same can be said for us. Jin S. Kim, the pastor of Church of All Nations in Minneapolis, writes of the seventh woe:

> In America, for example, people are fond of saying "our Founding Fathers" when discussing the admirable parts of history, but quickly exempt themselves from the genocide of Native Americans and the chattel slavery of African Americans. Brutality and inhumanity are also at the heart of our founding and history. Real leaders, according to Jesus take collective responsibility for the good and the bad.[2]

This is an important point, though we must be careful how we make use of it. Pastor Kim is right — good leaders must take responsibility for the good and the bad, but Christians have a history of using passages like this to demonize and brutalize Jews. So, keeping in mind the history of Christian interpretation of this passage, I'd like us to consider the meaning of the word hypocrite, which stands out in this barrage of woes.

I looked up the word "hypocrite," in the *Merriam-Webster's Online Dictionary*. They offer two primary definitions. First, a hypocrite is "a person who puts on a false appearance of virtue or religion." Second, a hypocrite is "a person who acts in contradiction to his or her stated beliefs or feelings." That is, a hypocrite is a person who isn't authentic. They hide their real identity behind

---

2   Jin S. Kim in *Feasting on the Gospels: Matthew Volume 2*, Cynthia A. Jarvis and E. Elizabeth Johnson, ed., (Louisville: Westminster John Knox Press, 2013), p. 222.

false piety. Consider that the prophet Amos pronounced judgment on Israel, because "they sell the righteous for silver, and the needy for a pair of sandals — they who trample the head of the poor into the dust of the earth, and push the afflicted out of the way" (Amos 2:6-7 NRSV). Yes, they are pretty on the outside, but dead on the inside.

Do you remember the story of the "BTK" serial killer? Over a period of nearly twenty years he tortured and murdered at least ten people. He also served as president of his congregation and as a Cub Scout leader. I don't think any of you are serial killers, but how can we know for sure?

I assure you that I'm not a serial killer, but as a religious leader I can identify with the Scribes and Pharisees. People tend to expect religious leaders to be pious, so hypocrisy or inauthenticity is a professional hazard. I know pastors who wouldn't dare go to the grocery story without wearing a tie and jacket, because they might run into a member of the congregation. Sometimes religious leaders feel like they have to put on a spiritual mask, because "being yourself" might not be acceptable. I try my best to be authentic, but I don't reveal everything — not even on Facebook.

So what Word does God want us to hear from this passage of scripture?

Franciscan priest and author Richard Rohr offers a helpful word in his book *Immortal Diamond*. He talks about the difference between the "true self" and the "false self." The "true self" has to do with the soul, which is "who you are in God and who God is in you."[3] This "true self" begins with our "divine DNA," or inner destiny. It's what makes us who we are, and it's a gift from God. We don't create it or earn it, but we must uncover it.

Unfortunately, we tend to take short cuts. We don't give our "true self" room to emerge and blossom. Instead we put on masks and present that face to the world, because we think that's what those around us want to see. So, when it comes to religion, we put on a pious face. That face, however, is our "false self."

---

3   Richard Rohr, *Immortal Diamond: The Search for Our True Self.* (San Francisco: Jossey-Bass, 2013), p. 16.

Now, we all have a "false self." Richard Rohr calls this our "small self." It's our "launching pad," and it includes body image, job, education, clothes, money, car, sexual identity, and success — just to name a few. "These are," he writes, "the trappings of ego that we all use to get through an ordinary day?" (p. 28). The false self isn't necessarily bad or evil; it's just less than our real identity.

Now, I need to say that neither Richard Rohr nor Jesus is suggesting that we just let it all hang out. This isn't permission to say to say whatever you want, whenever you want. Remember Paul said that while "all things are lawful, but not all things are beneficial" (1 Corinthians 10:23).

Rohr wrote that the "false self" is our "launching pad." It's where we start, but hopefully, as we mature in faith, though not necessarily in age, this false self will begin to die away. That is, as we grow in faith, we can put aside the mask of piety. Paul said something similar about the veil that Moses used to cover his face. He had originally used it because his face was so radiant it blinded people, but he kept it on long after it faded, because he was afraid they would think less of him (2 Corinthians 3:13).

This Lenten journey that we are embarking upon is an invitation to do a bit of self-examination. In the seven woes, Jesus invites us to look behind the veil, so we can find our true self and let go of the false self.

Why should we do this? At a time when growing numbers of people are either walking away from the church or just avoiding it all together — especially younger adults — one of the biggest complaints is that religious people — that's us — are hypocrites. Or, to put it a bit differently, people are looking for authenticity, and they don't seem to be finding it among self-professed religious people — especially in the church. Now, it's true that authenticity is difficult to nail down. But, the question is — when people look at us, do they see God in our lives? Do they see compassion, love, and grace, or do they see judgmentalism and self-righteousness?

The good news is that in Jesus, God has shown us grace, so that we might emerge from behind the veil and let the light that is Christ shine through us.

Preached March 9, 2014 (First Sunday of Lent)

CHAPTER 2
NO SIGNS FOR YOU

Matthew 12:38-42

When I plan out my sermon schedule, I decide upon a text and then try to come up with a good title. When I actually sit down to write the sermon, sometimes a few months later, the direction the sermon takes may have changed. So, when I read this passage, a famous phrase from *Seinfeld* came to mind. Remember the Soup Nazi? He made great soup, but he was very particular about how you ordered the soup. If you ruffled his feathers, he would say: "No soup for you!"

In reading this passage some months ago, I heard Jesus saying to the religious leaders in his audience, who came to him asking for a sign, "No signs for you." What I originally heard in this text was the demand that many make on people of faith to prove the existence of God. That can be a very intellectual pursuit. Theologians and philosophers from Anselm to Aquinas to Kant have expended a lot of energy trying to prove that God exists. And when they're done, the God they offer us can be abstract and lifeless. It's hard to have a relationship with the "Ground of Being."

In this case, the religious leaders weren't demanding proof that God exists. They wanted proof that Jesus spoke for God. They wanted confirmation, which would include miraculous deeds like healings. It's not that Jesus didn't offer them signs; they just weren't satisfied with the ones he'd given them. Since Matthew isn't shy about offering up miracle stories, I can hear in this passage an impatient Jesus asking these inquisitors: "What more do you want?" Only an evil generation keeps coming back wanting more evidence. You have enough evidence, so make your choice — will it be God or not?"

That is part of the story, but there's more to it than that. Jesus points us to two biblical stories. First, there's Jonah and Nineveh. Then there's the story of the Queen of Sheba. Jonah is the reluctant prophet who ends up in Nineveh, preaching to a people he despises, only to see them repent and follow God. As for the Queen of Sheba, she comes to Solomon, seeking wisdom - a wisdom that Solomon's own sons rejected. Now, standing before them is a person greater than either Jonah or Solomon. If Nineveh answered the call and the Queen of Sheba answered the call, why can't they heed his voice?

Once again, we need to be careful in how we read this passage. It's very easy to read it in an anti-Jewish manner. We can find ourselves blaming the Jews for not believing in Jesus, while Gentiles embraced him. If we can steer clear of that kind of interpretation, this passage may have something important to say to us.

Last week we talked about self-examination. That is an important part of our Lenten journey — looking inside, underneath the masks we all put on. In this reading, we hear a question about our ability and willingness to hear the voice of God. Can we, as Christians, become complacent and fail to heed the voice of God? Or, are we looking for signs in the sky?

Jesus isn't interested in engaging in "apologetics" — trying to prove God exists. Arguing with the likes of Richard Dawkins isn't a pressing concern. While there still are plenty of "cultured despisers" out there, the more pressing concern today is whether the church has something valuable to say about God.

Rather than look to the philosophers, we might want to look at someone like Pope Francis. He just celebrated the one year anniversary of his election to the papacy, and over the past year he has changed the face of the Catholic Church. It doesn't matter what your religion is — Francis has inspired people with his warmth, his compassion, his humanness.

There is a lot of concern in Christian circles about the decline of the church. Increasing numbers of people, especially younger people, have either left the church or ignore it. Most of the folks who fit into the category that survey-takers call "the Nones" don't reject the idea of God's existence. Many of them are quite spiritual in orientation. They just don't see the value in religious institutions, especially ones that they think exclude people because of their ethnicity, their socioeconomic status, their gender, or their sexual orientation.

Forty years ago, church growth gurus declared that conservative churches were growing because they had very definite doctrines and expectations. It is true that many conservative churches grew by making very clear distinctions about what they believed was true and what was false. But, that's changing. It's not that liberal churches are growing, but conservative ones have begun to see decline in their numbers, especially among people under forty.

Why are the churches experiencing decline? Well, liberal churches fell into the trap of privatizing their faith so they wouldn't offend anyone. They embraced the idea that religion, like politics, isn't appropriate in polite company. Conservative churches have begun to decline because their message no longer resonates. It's too narrow and harsh. Many people simply aren't attracted to places that claim to have all the answers, deny scientific truths, limit the roles of women, and exclude people because of their sexual orientation.

One of the reasons why Pope Francis is so popular, especially among younger people, whether Catholic or not, is because he exudes a sense of openness to the world. His decision to live in a monastery rather than the papal apartments, or his decision to wear ordinary shoes rather than red papal shoes, are signs that he gets the concern about hypocrisy among Christians.

I recently finished reading a book by Ken Wilson entitled *A Letter to My Congregation*. Ken is the pastor of the Vineyard Church in Ann Arbor. What is important about this book, and Ken's ministry, is that he has come to the conclusion that the church is called to fully embrace gay, lesbian, and transgender people. What makes the book and the ministry somewhat unique is that he is an evangelical. He came to this understanding in large part due to his pastoral work, which led him to rethink his interpretation of scripture and beliefs about gay folk. He began meeting with parents whose children are gay and lesbian, as well as gay and lesbian Christians. They wanted to know — does God love me for who I am? Besides the pastoral side of things, there was the missional element. He realized that his congregation, though it did pretty well reaching out to younger people — it's very contemporary in its worship — the congregation was aging. He realized that in a place like Ann Arbor, having a policy that excluded people who are gays undermined the mission of the church. Wilson concluded:

> Causing an unnecessary disincentive to follow Christ is a serious offense, at least as serious as failing to uphold a moral good. It would be easy to ignore or dismiss this concern if I didn't think it had substantial merit.[4]

The way the church treats LGBT people is only one issue among many. There are also issues of science and climate change, along with the plight of the poor, the immigrant, and the disabled.

Years ago the movie, *The Elephant Man*, made a significant impression on me. The movie tells the story of John Merrick. Like many films this one takes considerable license, even changing Merrick's name from Joseph to John. One of the most compelling moments of the film came when Dr. Treves, who had come to examine this man who society saw as a freak and even a monster, overheard John reciting Psalm 23. What made this remarkable was that Dr. Treves believed that John was so intellectually disabled that he couldn't speak. What was the message that I heard? It was that a man whom society considered expendable and an object of disgust was in truth a man of great intelligence and compassion. I heard in it the message that we should always value people, no matter their intellectual capacity, their looks, or their ethnicity. It would take me much longer before I could add sexual orientation to that list.

Although there are those who struggle with intellectual questions about the Christian faith, more often than not, the questions that inquirers have on their hearts and minds have more to do with our behavior. As Stacey Simpson Duke, another Ann Arbor pastor, puts it: "We do not need more evidence; we are the evidence." It is "our regenerated lives" that "are the sign of Jonah: Christ crucified and raised."[5] Yes, that is the only sign we need!!

Preached March 16, 2014 (Second Sunday of Lent)

4   Ken Wilson, *A Letter to My Congregation: An Evangelical Pastor's Path to Embracing People, lesbian and transgender into the Company of Jesus,* (Canton, MI: Read the Spirit Books, 2014), p. 50
5   Stacy Simpson Duke, *Feasting on the Gospels—Matthew, Volume 1,* p. 336.

CHAPTER 3

A TIME TO WEEP

Luke 19:41-44

> *For everything there is a season, and a time for every matter*
> *under heaven. There is: A time to weep, and a time to laugh;*
> *A time to mourn, and a time to dance.* (Ecclesiastes 3:1, 4 NRSV)

For Jesus, as he stood on the hillside overlooking Jerusalem, it was a time to weep. There is another occasion in the Gospel of Luke, where Jesus weeps over the city of Jerusalem. When a group of Pharisees comes to warn him of a plot to kill him, he laments Jerusalem's habit of killing the prophets and stoning those sent to it. Jesus declares that he wanted to "gather your children together as a hen gathers her brood under her wings, and you were not willing" (Luke 14:31-35).

Five chapters later, as the procession into Jerusalem we call Palm Sunday is underway, Jesus stops to take in the view. There, lying in front of him is the city of David. Standing in the center of the city is the Temple that Herod rebuilt and expanded into one of the ancient world's greatest wonders, making Jerusalem an important site of pilgrimage and commerce. Jesus should be happy. He should be rejoicing. But as he looks out at the city, he begins to weep, because the city is unable to recognize the presence of God in its midst. Therefore, they will choose a path that leads not to peace or justice, but destruction.

By the time that Luke writes this Gospel, the city of Jerusalem and its Temple will lie in ruins. The wars against the Romans that lasted from 66 to 70 CE ended with the destruction of the city and its Temple. But, it didn't have to happen this way. Unfortunately, the people chose the wrong way and suffered the consequences.

When Jesus weeps over the city, this isn't merely an emotional response at a perceived loss. This is a lament, which is, according to Fred Craddock:

A voice of love and profound caring, a vision of what could have been and of grief over its loss, of tough hope painfully releasing the object of his hope, of personal responsibility and frustration, of sorrow and anger mixed, of accepted loss but with energy enough to go on.[6]

As Jesus continued the procession into the city, he ends up in the Temple, where he overturns the tables of the religious marketers hoping to profit off of the people's piety. Of course, before long Jesus will be arrested, tried, convicted, and executed. Thus, another troublemaker will be out of the way. Except that's not the end of the story.

The reason that Jesus weeps is that the city seems blind to the presence of sin in its midst and its need for repentance. He weeps because the residents don't seem able to recognize God's presence. And that inability will have disastrous consequences.

That was then, but what about now? What word does Jesus have for us this morning?

In reflecting on this passage this past week, my thoughts went to the city in which we all live. And by city I mean the entire metro-Detroit region — on both sides of the divide between Detroit and its suburbs. Two weeks ago we gathered at First United Methodist Church of Birmingham to participate in the *Metro Coalition of Congregation's Action Assembly*. During this assembly we heard updates and calls to action on the issues of health care, immigration, human trafficking, and regional transit. We heard stories about real life people caught up in modern day slavery. We heard stories about a broken immigration system and a health care system that works well for some, but not for many others. We also heard updates on the efforts to finally create a truly regional transit system for Metro-Detroit. In our time together, we asked the question — what would God have us do?

A few days after this assembly, Pastor Louise Ott, Justin Erickson, and I met with Oakland County's Deputy Executive. We wanted to get his sense of where regional transit is going. We want-

---

6   Fred Craddock, *Luke: Interpretation*, (Louisville: Westminster John Knox Press, 1990), p. 229

ed to know where the roadblocks are and how we can help remove them. I'm pleased to say that it was a productive meeting. We even offered our churches as sites for town halls in preparation for the upcoming SMART millage vote.

What I heard from our Scripture this week is that Jesus weeps over the city. Although Detroit has a grand history, there has long been a dark lining to this history. Back when Edgar DeWitt Jones first came to town in 1920, Reinhold Niebuhr was serving as pastor of Bethel Evangelical Church. Although Niebuhr would leave Detroit in 1928 for Union Theological Seminary, where he became one of America's leading theologians and social ethicists, during his time here he spoke out clearly against the presence of injustice in the city. He also spoke against the complicity of the churches in this injustice.

During his time in Detroit, Niebuhr kept a journal, which he published after his move to New York. It's called *Leaves from the Notebook of a Tamed Cynic.* As he served Bethel Evangelical Church, he became disturbed by the inhumane conditions endured by the factory workers building cars for a growing middle class. He was also disturbed by the unwillingness of the city's clergy to stand with the unions in pursuing better wages and more humane working conditions.

He wrote this in 1926:

> I wish that some of our romanticists and sentimentalists could sit through a series of meetings where the real social problems of a city are discussed. They would be cured of their optimism. A city which is built around a productive process and which gives only casual thought and incidental attention to its human problems is really a kind of hell. Thousands in this town are really living in torment while the rest of us eat, drink and make merry. What a civilization.[7]

Jesus wept over the city of Jerusalem because it failed to heed the voice of God. On this day in March, as we continue our Lenten journey, what is Jesus saying to us? What responsibility do we

---

7   Niebuhr, Reinhold (2013-04-16). *Leaves from the Note Book of a Tamed Cynic.* (Kindle Locations 1133-1136).

have for changing the realities of our neighborhood, so that it is not "a kind of hell" where "thousands in this town are really living in torment?"

The causes of this hellishness might be different today than in Niebuhr's day, but I believe that Jesus continues to weep over cities, states, nations. Wherever injustice is present, where war rather than peace reigns, Jesus will weep. So how should we respond?

On another occasion Niebuhr wrote an entry that may have reflected frustration from being at too many conferences where religious leaders talked about doing the right thing, but never moving toward action.

Sermon after sermon, speech after speech is based upon the assumption that the people of the church are committed to the ethical ideals of Jesus and that they are the sole or at least chief agents of redemptive energy in society.

It was Niebuhr's complaint that too often we stay with general ideas and don't move toward specifics. Of course, when it comes to offering specifics:

> If that suggestion is made, the answer is that such a policy would breed contention. It certainly would. No moral project can be presented and no adventure made without resistance from the traditionalist and debate among experimentalists.

Niebuhr was a realist. He was also a doer. It wasn't enough to talk about ideals when there's work to be done. Yes, there might be resistance. The preacher might get some flack. But we must move to specifics. That was the message that Martin Luther King gave to white clergy as he sat in a Birmingham jail. Now was the time for action.

Detroit is in trouble, but so are the suburbs. The trouble may not seem immediate out here, but we're all in this together. One of the possible bridges to a new day for the people of Metro-Detroit is the creation of a truly effective and affordable public transit system. It will benefit young adults who want to live in the city. It will also help residents of both the city and the suburbs get to their jobs in an efficient and effective manner. It's even friendly to the environment.

The question is: Do we hear Jesus weeping over our communities? If we do, can we hear with him the voices of those crying out to God, pleading for deliverance? In this there is a pathway to God's peace and justice in the world.

Preached March 23, 2014 (Third Sunday of Lent)

CHAPTER 4

DIFFICULT PATHS

Mark 10:32-34

Jesus took the lead on their journey toward Jerusalem. Perhaps he was in a hurry to get there, but the disciples lagged behind. They seem to be caught up in the moment. It could be that this was their first visit to Jerusalem. There in front of them was the big city and the Temple. They'd heard about this Temple many times, and when they saw it in real life, it seemed even grander than they had ever imagined. Remember they didn't have cameras back then, so they had to use their imaginations to picture it. But it wasn't just the grandeur of the Temple that grabbed them. There were also the rumors that a violent fate awaited Jesus in Jerusalem. Jesus had even brought up the subject himself. So, it's no wonder that they wanted to take their time getting to Jerusalem. Because they didn't know what lay ahead of them, they were filled with mixed emotions — both amazement and fear.

When Jesus realizes that a gap was beginning to form, he stops and takes the twelve off to the side. Then, for the third time, Jesus explains to them that path before them would be difficult. He doesn't pull any punches. Yes, "the Son of Man will be handed over to the chief priests and the scribes, and they will condemn him to death; then they will hand him over to the Gentiles; they will mock him, and spit on him, and flog him, and kill him." If you were a disciple and you heard that message — how would you respond? Would you stay with Jesus or would you walk away? Amazingly they stay with him.

Perhaps it's the glimmer of a promise of resurrection that emboldens them to continue, or it may be that they took comfort in their earlier hopes that Jesus would take power in Jerusalem.

As Mark tells the story, it didn't take long before the disciples began to dream big dreams. Remember what James and John asked Jesus for? They asked Jesus to appoint them to leading posts in his new administration. "When you take over in Jerusalem could you put us in charge of the Departments of State and Defense? We don't want to be the one who gets left back at the office when you go down to the Capitol to deliver the state of the realm address." Of course, when the others hear of their audacity, they want to get into the act also. After all, no one wants to be the last one picked! (Mark 10:35-45). Yes, they quickly forget Jesus' warning — after all who is going to sign up for a mission is sure to fail? And so they clung to their vision of God's realm — one in which they got to have the seats of honor.

As I pondered this text and its message for us as a congregation, I thought about the many difficult paths that members of this congregation have taken in recent months and years.

Some of you have experienced a death in the family: A child, a sibling, a spouse, or a parent. Whether expected or not, death can be a wrenching experience for us.

For others of you, this difficult path involves a battle with cancer. Others of you are undergoing tests to see if cancer is present, and if it is then what treatments can be prescribed. Then there are the chronic illnesses, like Parkinson's. Others deal with mental health issues, something that we find difficult to talk about openly. For others it's the daily challenge posed by the aging process — including dealing with chronic pain.

Some among us have found that reaching mid-life has been difficult. A rough economy has led to job losses, along with the difficulties finding a new job, and the fear that retirement will bring unforeseen financial challenges. Besides these challenges, many "middle-aged" folks live sandwiched between concerns about both parents and children.

Many young adults have found themselves saddled with student debt and difficulty launching into their careers. They have their degrees, but jobs are scarce in an age of economic stagnation.

I think I've covered most everyone in this church. The challenges may differ from person to person, family to family, but as a community of faith, we have faced housing crises, job crises, health crises, and relationship crises. Some of our families have dealt with multiple issues. As a pastor, I often stand in awe of the resilience I see in some of your lives. The answer you all give is that it is prayer and the support of the community of faith that keeps you going.

It is in the context of these difficult pathways that are common to us all that I chose to view Jesus' own path to the cross. To put it in the words of a Robert Johns hymn:

> *In suff'ring love the thread of life is woven through our care,*
> *for God is with us: Not alone our pain and toil we bear.*

The hymn closes:

> *In suff'ring love our God comes now, hopes vision born in gloom;*
> *with tears and laughter shared and blessed the desert yet will bloom.*
> *In suffering love, God comes to us, bringing hope in the midst of*
> *gloom.*[8]

The message that I hear from Mark's text is that God in Christ understands the challenges we face. In his own experiences of suffering, Jesus brings healing to our souls. From the earliest of times the church has interpreted Jesus' journey to the cross through the lens of Isaiah 53, one of the Suffering Servant songs.

> *Surely he has borne our infirmities and carried our diseases;*
> *yet we accounted him stricken, struck down by God, and afflicted.*
> *But he was wounded for our transgressions, crushed for our iniquities;*
> *upon him was the punishment that made us whole, and by his*
> *bruises we are healed.*   (Isaiah 53:4- 5 NRSV).

In embracing the way of the cross, this servant of servants shares in our experiences of suffering. He bears the effects of our transgressions and our iniquities. And as he does so, he brings us healing and makes us whole.

As we read the New Testament, it's clear that the early Christians connected the cross to our salvation. This has led some to believe that God punishes Jesus instead of us — sort of like kicking the dog instead of the child when the child misbehaves. As I read these texts, I see something different. I see in Jesus, God working to bring healing to our brokenness. I see humanity throwing everything it can at Jesus, and Jesus overcoming our resistance to his offer

---

8   *Chalice Hymnal,* (St. Louis: Chalice Press, 1995), 212.

of reconciliation. The key to this interpretation is the message of Easter. Good Friday will have its say, but it won't have the last word.

Although one particular understanding of the cross has dominated Protestant thought for generations, there are a number of ways of understanding the cross. Mark 10, for instance, offers a ransom theory of the atonement, with Jesus speaking of himself as that ransom. In traditional ransom theologies, Jesus gives his life to the devil in exchange for our lives. He does this because we sold our souls to the devil. There is something of this theory in C.S. Lewis' *The Lion, the Witch, and the Wardrobe*. Remember how Aslan gives his life to the White Witch in exchange for Edmund's life. Of course, as you might remember, death cannot contain Aslan, who comes back to life because there is a deeper magic that the White Witch didn't know about. Of course, it's interesting that Mark doesn't name the recipient of this ransom payment. Instead, we're simply told that Jesus has given his life "to liberate many people" (Mark 10:45 CEB).

There's another atonement theory that I think fits our conversation this morning. Back in the second century, Irenaeus developed what has come to be known as the recapitulation theory. In this theory of the atonement, as Jesus goes through life — from birth to death — he undoes the damage we create in the course of our lives. In other words, by living faithfully in relationship with God, Jesus overcomes our resistance to God's promises and expectations. In his life, as well as his death, Jesus perfects our imperfections — bringing us to maturity of faith. This is a difficult journey, because it will involve a violent death, but death is part of our journey toward God. Death is of course, the last enemy to be overcome. So, in Irenaeus' vision, by dying on a tree, Jesus reverses the disobedience of Adam who ate from the forbidden tree.[9]

As we make our way down the path of life, we will experience times of great difficulty. But the good news is that Jesus has walked this path before. He understands our situation. He knows our suffering, and therefore God knows our suffering.

---

9   Cyril C. Richardson, *Early Christian Fathers*, (New York: Macmillan Pub., 1970), p. 389

But the key to this journey is found in the last half of verse 34: "after three days he will rise again." It's this promise of the resurrection that gives us hope, because in the resurrection death loses its sting. In the resurrection every tear is wiped away and death will be no more (Revelation 21:4). This is the promise that sustains us in season and out of season.

Preached March 30, 2014 (Fourth Sunday of Lent)

CHAPTER 5

BE ALERT

Mark 13:21-23

A little over a week ago Fred Phelps died. If you don't know who Fred Phelps is, he led a small fringe Baptist church in Topeka, Kansas. Fred and his church, which is composed mostly of family members, are well known for picketing religious gatherings and funerals, especially military funerals. They have a two-pronged message — "God hates fags" and "God hates America." I first encountered them when we were living in Kansas. It seemed like every Saturday that we went to Topeka, they were just finishing up their protest march at the local shopping mall. I'd never heard of them until I got to Kansas in 1995, but since then they've become an increasingly visible presence across the country. They claim to represent God, but do they?

Many claim to be prophets, but how do you know who speaks the truth? Does the message of hate proclaimed by the Phelps family represent the message Jesus proclaimed? Or, are they simply the most visible expressions of what Martin Thielen calls "Bad Religion?"

Some of you might recognize Pastor Thielen's name, since our study groups once used his book *What's the Least I Can Believe and Still Be a Christian?* Now he has a new book with the title: *The Answer to Bad Religion Is Not No Religion.*

Because the gospel of Jesus gets drowned out by negative and hateful messages offered in the name of God, many in our society find the message of a famous John Lennon song attractive:

> *Imagine there's no heaven, it's easy if you try.*
> *No Hell below us, above us only sky.*
> *Imagine all the people living for today*
> *Imagine there's no countries, It isn't hard to do*
> *Nothing to kill or die for*
> *And no religion, too*
> *Imagine all the people, living life in peace*

If only there were no countries and no religions — then we could live in peace.

But, must we abandon religion if we're going to live in peace? Speaking only as a Christian, is my faith defined by the likes of Fred Phelps and others like him?

Jesus warns us about false messiahs who claim to represent God. He tells us that even if they perform signs and wonders don't follow them. Instead, be alert to the voice of God that calls out to us. In this call for discernment, Jesus tells us that he has already taught us everything we need to know to distinguish between bad and good religion.

In Mark 13 Jesus offers us an apocalyptic vision. Like the Book of Revelation, this much briefer apocalypse puts things into perspective. His message to the disciples is simple — don't put your trust in buildings like the Temple they had been admiring or in nationalistic movements that continually arose in Roman-occupied Palestine. These buildings will be destroyed, and these movements will fail. Mark even puts in a little note reminding his readers that the Jewish Wars, which had occurred not long before this gospel was written, had left the city of Jerusalem and its Temple in ruins and its nationalist messiahs lay dead. That is not the way of the Gospel. Yes, Jesus will suffer death, but Easter will also come, and with it comes a new community — an alternative community that will exhibit the values and vision of God's realm.

So beware of the scam artists pretending to represent God. Like those computer-generated calls that tell you that your car warranty has run out and invite you to re-up — just hang up! If it sounds too good to be true, then it probably is. They may perform signs and wonders, but don't let them fool you. These are just tricks designed to deceive you.

There is bad religion and there is good religion.

According to Martin Thielen, bad religion is self-righteous. It's also chronically negative. That is, it's always complaining. It can't find anything good to say about anyone or anything. It's also arrogant and intolerant. It's partisan and nationalist. As Disciple theologian Joe Jones puts the question:

"Am I an American who happens to be a Christian, or am I a Christian who happens to be an American? *Which identity orders which?*"[10] How we answer that question will help determine the nature of our faith. Finally, bad religion is nominalistic. That is — it allows time for God and church when it's convenient.

There are many other elements that we could add to the list, but this gets the point across. If this is what people think religion is, then it's no wonder they opt out of "institutional religion." With religions like that, there will never be peace on earth, or good will to all!

But, is this the only option? Is it possible that there is a good form of religion? Thankfully Martin Thielen offers just such a list that ranges from engaging in service to others to having an open mind, from prioritizing love to promoting gratitude. These expressions of good religion affect the way we live our daily lives — not only on Sunday for an hour or two.

The way to good religion depends on who and what guides our lives. It speaks to the way we make our decisions? And it defines our witness to our neighbors.

In Mark 13, Jesus tells us that he has given us the instructions we need to live before God. That message echoes one we find in Deuteronomy 13.

> *The Lord your God you shall follow, him alone shall you fear, his commandments you shall keep, his voice you shall obey, him shall you serve, and to him shall you hold fast.* (Deuteronomy 13:4).

There are many voices calling out to us. Not all of them are specifically religious. But these are competing voices. The question is — to whom will you listen?

Jesus invites us to be people of discernment. He invites us to look at our lives through the lens of the Gospel. It's not just the religious dimensions of life, but the entirety of our lives — our jobs, our volunteer efforts, the cars we drive, the way we vote. As we prayerfully seek a way forward, we will need to train ourselves to

---

10   Joe R. Jones, *A Lover's Quarrel: A Theologian and His Beloved Church*, (Eugene, OR: Cascade Books, 2014).

filter out all the extraneous noise that can distract us from hearing God, who often speaks to us in a still and soft voice. But Jesus tells us that we have everything we need to discern God's voice. We can know the difference between bad and good religion. We just have to follow the voice of Jesus.

We value diversity of opinion in this congregation. It's a core value that we trace back to the founding days of the Stone-Campbell Movement. It's part of our creed — our orthodoxy. But, this sense of freedom needs to be tempered by an attentive ear to God's voice that comes to us through Christ our Lord.

Our tradition, as theologian Joe Jones puts it, has often embraced a worldly creed that declares: "Nobody can tell me what I ought to believe; it is my own private decision." But, is this true? If Jesus is Lord then what does that mean in our context?[11]

How we answer the question about the Lordship of Christ will determine whether we embrace a bad form or a good form of religion. How we answer will determine our witness to the world. As Paul writes to the Thessalonians:

> *Rejoice always, pray without ceasing, give thanks in all circumstances; for this is the will of God in Christ Jesus for you. Do not quench the Spirit. Do not despise the words of prophets, but test everything; hold fast to what is good; abstain from every form of evil.* (1 Thessalonians 5:16-22).

Preached April 6, 2014 (Fifth Sunday of Lent)

---

11 Jones, *Lover's Quarrel*, p. 57.

Chapter 6

Time's Up

John 16:16-33

March Madness should be a fading memory by now, but those of you who pay attention to such things know that when the buzzer sounds, the game is over. If a ball enters the basket before time runs out, it counts. That last second shot might even win the game. But, if the ball goes through the basket just a half a second after the buzzer sounds — then it's of no consequence. The game is over, and the team with the highest score gets the win.

In matters spiritual, our Lenten journey has reached the final minutes. The buzzer is about to sound. We've had our procession. We've sung Hosanna and King of Kings, while waving palm branches. We've even heard the children remind us to be happy in Jesus. But that's all in the past. Now we must face a future that is defined by the road to the cross. You might say — the clock is ticking.

By the time we come to the moment recorded in John 16, the meal is over, Jesus has washed the disciples' feet, and now he's giving final instructions to his disciples. He's been telling them that his time is short; that he will be leaving them, but he won't leave them alone. He will send the Comforter to be with them. He understands their reluctance to let go of him. He understands their grief. They had high hopes for their future with Jesus, but now Jesus is telling them that he must go away. His time is up. The buzzer is about to sound.

This passage is rich in eschatological meaning. For John, Jesus' death, burial, and resurrection mark the transition from one age to another. As Paul puts it in 2 Corinthians 5, the old is gone, and the new has arrived. But, letting go isn't easy.

I've been going through some of my books because my shelves are full. I need to make room for my recent acquisitions, but even if I've not read some of these books in years — if I even read them — it's difficult to let go of them. Many of us have a lot invested in the old age. So, saying goodbye is difficult, even if what lies on the other side will bring blessings.

So, here we are — the game clock is ticking, and we're out of time-outs. We're a point behind, and there's just enough time to get one last shot off. If it goes in we win; if not, we lose. But, as Cub fans put it: there's always next year!

One of the reasons why we hang onto the old is because we're not sure about what lies on the other side. We know what we already have, but the future is unknown to us. So, the temptation is to play it safe and stick with what we know. You remember how the Hebrews, after they escaped slavery in Egypt, began to pine for the old life in Egypt. It wasn't a great life — being a slave and all — but freedom in Sinai didn't seem like much of an improvement. After all, they were running low on bread and the water. Better to be a slave than dead in the desert.

So, you can understand why the disciples aren't thrilled with the news that Jesus is about to depart from them. They like things the way they are. They don't want to say goodbye, even if they will meet him on the other side.

You won't find too many parables in John's gospel, but John records one in this passage. It's a story that some of you can resonate with — it has to do with the painfulness of childbirth. This isn't the first time that Jesus has talked about the birth process. Remember how he invited Nicodemus to be born again? Do you also remember how Nicodemus struggled to make sense of Jesus' words? How is this possible? He asked. In John 16, the time for new birth has arrived.

As a male, I don't have firsthand experience with being pregnant or being in labor. Although I was there when Brett was born, I didn't experience Cheryl's labor pains. But I do know that there is unspeakable joy on the far side of these labor pains. Part of this joy is simply relief from the often painful process of giving birth. Still, there is also joy in realizing that a new age is dawning. Even a father, who hasn't experienced the pain of child birth, gets to experience that kind of joy.

Jesus invites us to consider his own death and resurrection to be a moment of new birth. Even if the process can be painful, there will be joy on the other side. It's not an easy path — for Jesus or for us. The disciples feel comfortable with the way things are. They still have their questions. They're not sure they're ready to go out on their own. But Jesus tells them — time is up. It's time to leave the old age behind and enter this new age that God has set before us. When we do this, then we'll find the answers we're looking for. Of course, going forward involves a great deal of faith and trust in God.

For John, the resurrection of Jesus is the central eschatological moment for the world. The new future begins at the moment of his resurrection. Having come from the Father, he must return to the Father. But, Jesus has already given us the promise of the Comforter — the Paraclete — who is always with us — revealing to us what we need to know as the people of God.

While it's difficult to let go of the old, the new beckons us. What is the old? It is what theologian Walter Wink called the Domination System — it's the system of violence and oppression that enslaves the world.[12] But in the death and resurrection of Jesus, that system — that world — has been conquered. It wasn't through an act of violence on the part of Jesus, but the victory came as Jesus overcame an act of violence — for death could not hold him. In the resurrection Jesus has broken the bonds of death — for him and for us. And in this there is joy — if we're willing to embrace it!

I was on the phone with a friend when the operator broke through and told me I had an emergency call. I'd never had an emergency call before, but I hung up the phone, and waited for that emergency call to come through. It was Cheryl's school. The person in the office told me that Cheryl had gone to the hospital because she was in labor. I wasn't ready for that call, so I insisted that it wasn't time. But apparently my clock and Brett's clock weren't in sync! He was ready to come into the world, but I wasn't sure — as a prospective father — whether I was ready.

12 See Walter Wink, *The Powers that Be: Theology for a New Millennium*, (New York: Doubleday, 1998).

The hour has come. The time of suffering is about to begin. The disciples will scatter, but Jesus won't be alone — the Father will be with him. This too will pass, for Jesus has conquered the world.

The world presses in on Jesus. The world, which God loves, causes his son to suffer and die, but, in the Resurrection, Jesus emerges as the victor. The Old Age — the Age of the Domination System — is no more. And, so the invitation goes out: Are you ready to enter the new age of God's peace and God's justice that began with the Resurrection?

Preached April 13, 2014 (Palm/Passion Sunday)

CHAPTER 7

UNBELIEVABLE NEWS

Mark 16:9-20

If you were reading along with Cheryl, did you notice the brackets around the morning's passage? They're a signal that these verses are a later addition to the Gospel of Mark. Because most scholars believe that Mark's Gospel ends with verse 8 and not verse 20, not too many sermons get preached from this text. I wouldn't have preached on it either, except I've been following an alternative set of readings during the Lenten season and this is the chosen text for Easter Sunday.

But even if this reading comes from a Second Century addition, could there still be a word from God present in these verses? After all, for many centuries this addition to the Gospel was considered sacred scripture — even the verses that talk about snakes and poison!

Mark 16 begins with a group of women going to the tomb to finish the burial process. As they walk to the tomb they begin to realize that they might have trouble moving the stone covering the entrance, so when they arrive, they're rather surprised to find that the stone has already been moved. When they look inside, they discover that Jesus' body is missing, but they do find a young man sitting off to the right side of the tomb. He tells them not to be afraid, but to go and tell Peter and the others that Jesus has been raised from the dead and will meet them in Galilee. Instead of going to Peter and telling him the news, they go home and keep this news to themselves. With that the Gospel of Mark ends.

If the Gospel of Mark does end in verse 8, as most scholars believe, you can understand why someone might want to add an epilogue to it. Having the women go home without sharing the news leaves you wanting more, doesn't it? It's like when I went to see Mel Gibson's *The Passion of the Christ*. I found myself unsettled and a bit bewildered by the brevity of the film's resurrection scene. We went from the violence of the crucifixion to a passing glance at the empty tomb, and then the credits rolled. As I sat there, rather numb, I wanted to write a different ending! And that's what happened here — someone decided to finish the story by drawing on scenes from the other three gospels.

There is something about this epilogue, however, that is somewhat unsettling. There are scenes here — like the handling of snakes and drinking of poison — that seem rather unbelievable. But then isn't the resurrection itself a bit unbelievable? After all, people just don't rise from the dead every day. For many people, the resurrection sounds like crazy talk.

Many people have tried to give "proof" that Jesus rose from the dead, but these efforts generally fall short. There were no cameras to record the event, and even the Gospels don't say much — they just tell us that he was seen alive by his disciples. But as a result, their lives seem to have been transformed. As I shared with a reporter from the Free Press, ultimately we have to take this news about the resurrection by faith. Not even an empty tomb is sufficient proof.[13]

As we read this epilogue, which was written sometime in the Second Century, to give closure to Mark's Gospel, we find Jesus appearing to Mary Magdalene, just like in John 20. When she goes and tells the disciples, who were mourning and weeping, that Jesus had risen, no one believes her. Why would they?

Then Jesus appears to two disciples who are on a trip into the countryside. You may notice some similarities to Luke's story of the encounter on the road to Emmaus. Jesus doesn't break bread with them, but he does tell them to go and share the news with the other disciples. And once again — no one will believe what seems like unbelievable news.

Finally, Jesus appears to the whole community, and he gives them a good talking-to. He asks them why they're being so stubborn in their unbelief. Why is this such unbelievable news? In answer to this question, I like the way Bruce Epperly puts it:

---

13 Niraj Warikoo, "Metro Detroit megachurch reaches out to doubters on Easter Sunday," *Detroit Free Press*, (http://www.freep.com/article/20140420/NEWS05/304200051)

The resurrection will always remain a mystery, hidden from rationalists, Enlightenment-thinkers, and literalists. It is always more than we can ask or imagine.[14]

Too often, when we try to explain the resurrection, we end up domesticating it. When we do this, we miss the deeper message. Bruce points us back to C.S. Lewis's *The Lion, the Witch and the Wardrobe.* The White Witch thought she had killed Aslan, but there was a deeper magic that she didn't understand. As a result Aslan was resurrected, and the Witch was defeated. We may not have all the answers, but something happened that first Easter morning that transformed the lives of Jesus' followers. There is a power present in the universe deeper than we can truly imagine, and that power is present in the Risen Christ.

Despite the unbelief of his disciples, Jesus isn't finished with them quite yet. They may struggle to make sense of the resurrection, like many of us do, but the message of the resurrection is still good news that needs to be proclaimed to the world.

Mirroring the message of Matthew 28, Jesus gives the disciples their commission: "Go into all the World and proclaim the good news to the whole creation." That is the key point in this passage. We have a message to share with the world. It might sound unbelievable to some, but it will be life changing for others. William Barclay offers four points of relevance in this passage for us today. First, "the church has a preaching task." We have a duty, he says, "to tell the story of the good news of Jesus to those who have never heard it." The second point is that "the church has a healing task." Remember that Jesus tells the disciples that they will "lay their hands on the sick, and they will recover." We see this happen on numerous occasions in the Book of Acts. It's clear from Scripture that God isn't just concerned about minds and souls. God is also concerned about bodies. Third, the "church has a source of power." We can easily get put off by references to snakes and poison and speaking in tongues, but as Barclay puts it — "at the back of this

---

14 Bruce Epperly, "Resurrection without Supernaturalism," *Living a Holy Adventure*, (http://www.patheos.com/blogs/livingaholyadventure/2014/04/resurrection-without-supernaturalism)

picturesque language is the conviction that the Christian is filled with a power to cope with life that others do not possess." Finally, "the church is never left alone to do its work." There is a promise here that "the Lord of the church is still in the church and is still the Lord of power."[15]

Therefore, there is no need to fear!

We began the service with an announcement of the Resurrection. In that announcement, he heard the promise that "Our story is an invitation to insurrection." And you responded: "Christ has risen! Christ has risen indeed!" And the announcement closed with the proclamation: Christ has risen! Let the resurrection insurrection begin! You responded: Christ has risen Indeed!

The news of the resurrection might seem unbelievable, but if we're willing to take a risk and follow the risen Christ into the heart of God, then we will get to participate in an insurrection that can change the world!

Alleluia — Christ the Lord is Risen!

Preached on April 20, 2014 (Easter Sunday)

---

15 William Barclay, *The Gospel of Mark (The New Daily Study Bible)*, Revised Edition, (Philadelphia: Westminster Press, 1975), pp. 370-371].

TOPICAL LINE DRIVES

Straight to the Point in under 44 Pages

All Topical Line Drives volumes are priced at $4.99 print and 99¢ in all ebook formats.

Available

The Authorship of Hebrews: The Case for Paul	David Alan Black
What Protestants Need to Know about Roman Catholics	Robert LaRochelle
What Roman Catholics Need to Know about Protestants	Robert LaRochelle
Forgiveness: Finding Freedom from Your Past	Harvey Brown, Jr.
Process Theology: Embracing Adventure with God	Bruce Epperly

Holistic Spirituality: Life Transforming Wisdom from the Letter of James
Bruce Epperly

To Date or Not to Date: What the Bible Says about Pre-Marital Relationships
D. Kevin Brown

The Eucharist: Encounters with Jesus at the Table	Robert D. Cornwall

The Authority of Scripture in a Postmodern Age: Some Help from Karl Barth
Robert D. Cornwall

Rendering unto Caesar	Chris Surber
The Caregiver's Beatitudes	Robert Martin
What is Wrong with Social Justice	Elgin Hushbeck, Jr.

Forthcoming

God the Creator: The Variety of Christian Views on Origins	Henry Neufeld
I'm Right and You're Wrong	Steve Kindle
Stewardship: God's Way of Recreating the World	Steve Kindle
Why Christians Should Care about Their Jewish Roots	Nancy Petrey
A Cup of Cold Water	Chris Surber
Words of Woe: Alternative Lectionary Texts	Robert D. Cornwall

Planned

Christian Existentialism	David Moffett-Moore
Paths to Prayer	David Moffett-Moore

(The titles of planned volumes may change before release.)

Generous Quantity Discounts Available
Dealer Inquiries Welcome
Energion Publications — P.O. Box 841
Gonzalez, FL 32560
Website: http://energionpubs.com
Phone: (850) 525-3916

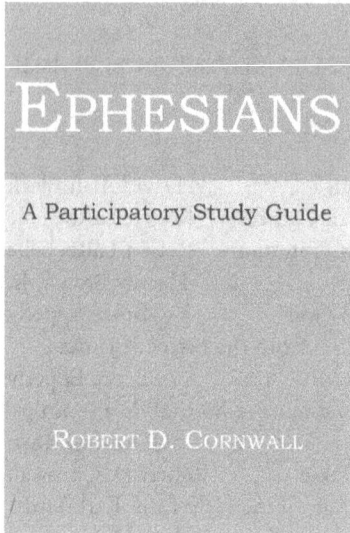

EPHESIANS

A Participatory Study Guide

ROBERT D. CORNWALL

Bob Cornwall combines the mind of a scholar and the heart of a pastor in this participatory study guide on Ephesians.

Dr. Glen Miles
Senior Minister
Country Club Christian Church
(Disciples of Christ)
Kansas City, MO

BY ROBERT D. CORNWALL

The time is now for mainline churches to reappropriate the full spectrum of the spiritual gifts for their contemporary tasks.

Amos Yong, Ph.D.
Dean
Divinity School
Regent University
Author of *Spirit of Love*

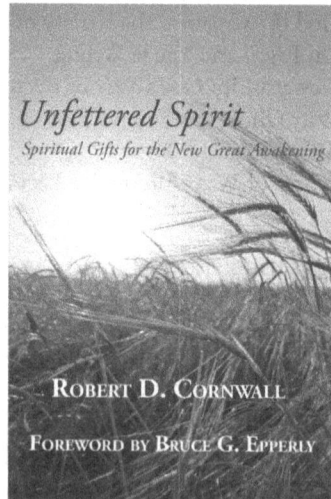

Unfettered Spirit
Spiritual Gifts for the New Great Awakening

ROBERT D. CORNWALL

FOREWORD BY BRUCE G. EPPERLY

More from Energion Publications

Personal Study

Finding My Way in Christianity	Herold Weiss	$16.99
The Jesus Paradigm	David Alan Black	$17.99
When People Speak for God	Henry Neufeld	$17.99

Christian Living

Faith in the Public Square	Robert D. Cornwall	$16.99
Grief: Finding the Candle of Light	Jody Neufeld	$8.99
Crossing the Street	Robert LaRochelle	$16.99

Bible Study

Learning and Living Scripture	Lentz/Neufeld	$12.99
From Inspiration to Understanding	Edward W. H. Vick	$24.99
Luke: A Participatory Study Guide	Geoffrey Lentz	$8.99
Philippians: A Participatory Study Guide	Bruce Epperly	$9.99
Ephesians: A Participatory Study Guide	Robert D. Cornwall	$9.99
Evidence for the Bible	Elgin Hushbeck, Jr.	

Theology

Creation in Scripture	Herold Weiss	$12.99
Creation: the Christian Doctrine	Edward W. H. Vick	$12.99
Ultimate Allegiance	Robert D. Cornwall	$9.99
History and Christian Faith	Edward W. H. Vick	$9.99
The Church Under the Cross	William Powell Tuck	$11.99
The Journey to the Undiscovered Country	William Powell Tuck	$9.99
Eschatology: A Participatory Study Guide	Edward W. H. Vick	$9.99
Philosophy for Believers	Edward W. H. Vick	$14.99
Christianity and Secularism	Elgin Hushbeck, Jr.	$16.99

Ministry

Clergy Table Talk	Kent Ira Groff	$9.99
So Much Older Then ...	Robert LaRochelle	$9.99

Generous Quantity Discounts Available
Dealer Inquiries Welcome
Energion Publications — P.O. Box 841
Gonzalez, FL 32560
Website: http://energionpubs.com
Phone: (850) 525-3916

www.ingramcontent.com/pod-product-compliance
Lightning Source LLC
Chambersburg PA
CBHW010039040426
42331CB00037B/3331